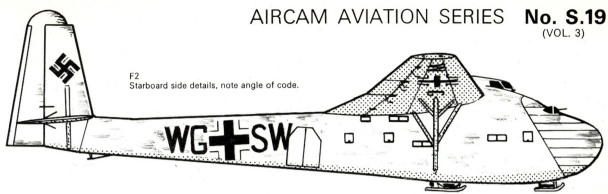

F2
Starboard side details, note angle of code.

AIRCAM AVIATION SERIES No S19 (VOL 3)

LUFTWAFFE
COLOUR SCHEMES & MARKINGS 1939-45
MAINLY WINTER SCHEMES

Bf 110; He 50A; Hs 123; Hs 129; Fw 189; Ju 87; Ju 88; He 111HPZ;
He 114; He 115; Ar 95; Ar 196; Bv 138; Do 24; Ju 52; Me 321.

Illustrated and compiled by Richard Ward

ACKNOWLEDGEMENTS

This, the third volume in the AIRCAM AVIATION SERIES on Luftwaffe Colour Schemes and Markings, illustrates in greater detail than the two previous volumes (S.6 and S.8) the temporary winter schemes applied to front line aircraft other than single-engined fighters. The winter schemes of both the Bf 109 and Fw 190 have been more than adequately covered in AIRCAM Nos. 39, 40, 42, 43 and 44. The next volume, No. S.20, will illustrate types not to be found in this book such as the Do 17Z, Hs 126, Fi 156, etc. in both winter and standard schemes. All photographs in this book are Bundesarchiv. Acknowledgement must be made to the published researches of Herr Karl Reis Jr.

F1
Starboard side details.

Published by: Osprey Publishing Limited, England
Editorial Office: P.O. Box 5, Canterbury, Kent, England
Subscription & Business Office: P.O. Box 25, 707 Oxford Road, Reading, Berkshire, England

The Berkshire Printing Co. Ltd.   © Osprey Publishing Ltd. 1974   ISBN 0 85045 277 5

The RAF had the Swordfish and the Luftwaffe also had its decrepids, above a pair of Heinkel He 50A's on the Eastern Front during the 1943–44 winter flown by Estonian aircrew with Nachtschlachtgruppe 11. The aircraft on the ground is 3W+NP as illustrated below and in colour side-view B1, note yellow 1 in yellow circle on rudder. 3W+NR similarly camouflaged carried a black circle with black 20 on all white rudder.

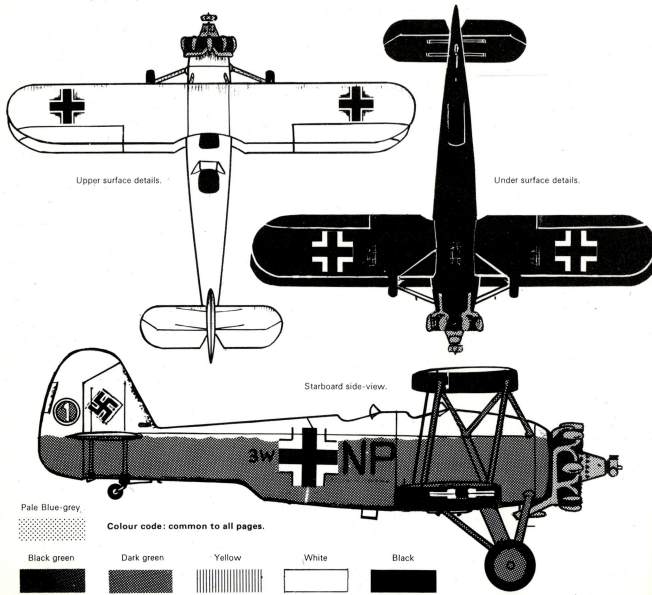

Upper surface details.

Under surface details.

Starboard side-view.

Pale Blue-grey

Colour code: common to all pages.

Black green   Dark green   Yellow   White   Black

Nose detail of Bf 110D-3 flown by Major Schulze-Dickow, Kommandeur of III./ZG 26, North Africa, Mediterranean area, 1941.

LUFTWAFFE
Colour Schemes & Markings 1939-45

Mainly Winter Schemes

Basic Camouflage

The text in this book relates to the camouflage and markings of Luftwaffe aircraft in general with the exception of single-engined fighters, the Messerschmitt Bf 109 and Focke-Wulf Fw 190 having been adequately covered in AIRCAM Nos. 39, 40, 42, 43 and 44.

The Luftwaffe went to war in 1939 in two basic camouflage schemes, the splinter scheme comprising black green (swarzgrün) and dark green (dunkelgrün) on the upper surfaces or upper surfaces in black green only, both with pale blue-grey (hellblau) under surfaces. The former scheme was the more common in late 1939 early 1940, the latter scheme coming into more general use as the war progressed, though never so common as the former. The first major change in the basic camouflage came towards the end of 1940 and was brought about through the crippling losses inflicted on Luftwaffe bomber formations by RAF fighters during their daylight attacks throughout the Battle of Britain period. With the eventual defeat of the Luftwaffe by day the bomber force was switched to night operations. With the change to night attack the pale blue-grey under surfaces were hastily covered with a coat of matt black and so far as the He 111 was concerned most of the aft fuselage between the trailing edge of the wings to the tail-plane to a line above the fuselage cross was also blacked in, as may be seen in colour side-views E1 and E2. The vertical tail surfaces were in many cases also given a coat of black often covering the swastika also. Upper surfaces were treated with a black squiggle pattern as were fuselage sides left in the basic scheme; national insignia on both upper and under surfaces were often either blacked out or roughly daubed over or the white angles painted in leaving just a thin white outline as illustrated in E1, 2 and 3 and on the cover background. The fuselage cross received the same treatment and in the majority of cases the code was reduced to the aircraft letter only, white and yellow letters often being blacked in leaving only a thin outline of the original colour. Wing letters were usually painted out though some units retained them. Colour side-view E3 illustrates the ultimate night scheme used by some units, overall matt black, though many aircraft received a black fuselage and under surfaces, the upper surfaces remaining in standard camouflage receiving black squiggles or blotches. Whilst the above remarks apply directly to the He 111 they are equally applicable to the Ju 88 though on the latter type the squiggle upper surfaces were not nearly so common. Whatever the directive issued by the Reichluftfartministerium regarding the night camouflage of bomber units, it was certainly very loosely interpreted at unit level in the early days, though eventually a standard scheme emerged for night operations which was to remain for the duration of the war. No. S.20 will illustrate such schemes.

Winter

The first temporary winter schemes were used by the Luftwaffe in Norway but apparently only on light liaison types such as the Fi 156. The first general application of white upper surfaces to all operational types came with the advent of the first winter in Russia, 1941–42. As with the matt black used in 1940, the matt white used in Russia was a water soluble based paint which quickly weathered, allowing streaks of the basic camouflage colour to appear in lesser or greater degree on leading edges, engine cowls and panel joins. The two most common applications were flat white as B6 and D2 or as F3, 4 and 5 where the density of white was varied, permitting

He 111 with black daubed under surfaces and snow upper surfaces, note the new aileron on the port wing. KG 53, Russia.

the camouflage to show through. The matt white was both a defensive and offensive scheme, especially on and over the featureless steppes in the dead of winter, but time of year and terrain brought many variations to the basic flat white. For example when the thaw came many units, especially ground-attack units, broke the shape of the aircraft by splotching white on the upper surfaces as in the case of side-views C5 and B4, 5. Apparently this scheme was also applied when dispersal areas were in heavy woodland. As a general rule canopy frames were left in the original scheme, though there are many exceptions to be found on all types of aircraft, an example being D4.

The Ju 87 units probably produced the greatest variety of finishes, varying from pristine white through delicate spray-gun squiggles to crudely hand brushed squiggles, streaks and blotches. These schemes will be well covered in the Ju 87 AIRCAM No. 46. Most He 111 units were satisfied with a flat white scheme in varying stages of weathering, though some broke up the upper surfaces with interesting variations as for example KG 51 and 53. Aircraft of both units are illustrated in colour in AIRCAM No. S.8. Some interesting colour combinations came into being in Russia on He 111's used on night operations as illustrated in side-view E4 and on the front cover. Both aircraft belong to KG 27 though KG 4 also used this scheme, as no doubt did other units, and probably both the above mentioned units daubed matt black over the complete under surfaces including the yellow theatre markings as illustrated in the photograph on this page. The Ju 88 illustrated in side-view D3 shows a very interesting and time-consuming application of a winter scheme as it was applied by a spray gun with a very fine nozzle in merging and near merging stripes producing the fine zebra effect.

Marine units based in Norway and operating over the Arctic convoy routes used a splotched scheme as illustrated in side-views D1 and 5. Photographic evidence indicates that this splotching was not applied to the upper surface of the wings and tail-plane of the majority of aircraft so camouflaged, though no doubt there were exceptions to the two types illustrated here; certainly at least one Bv 222 transport was blotched on the upper surfaces as well as the fuselage.

Me 321 in slightly weathered winter scheme probably on an airfield in the Bagerovo area in the Crimea where they were used on supply operations into the Kuban bridgehead towed by He 111Z's, one of which may be seen in the background, also in winter upper surfaces. Neither of these aircraft show any sign of yellow fuselage and wing tip theatre markings.

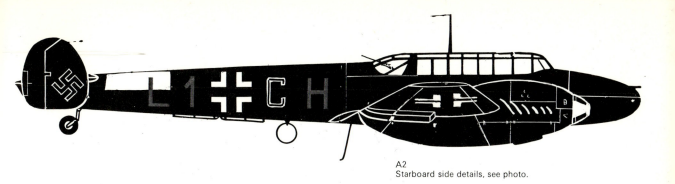

A2
Starboard side details, see photo.

Bf 110C-4 of ZG 1 in standard scheme, Russia 1941. Code is S9+EP.

Bf 110C-4 of II./SKG 210, Russia, winter 1941–42. This unit was formed from elements of III./ZG 1 hence the "Wespen" insignia on nose.

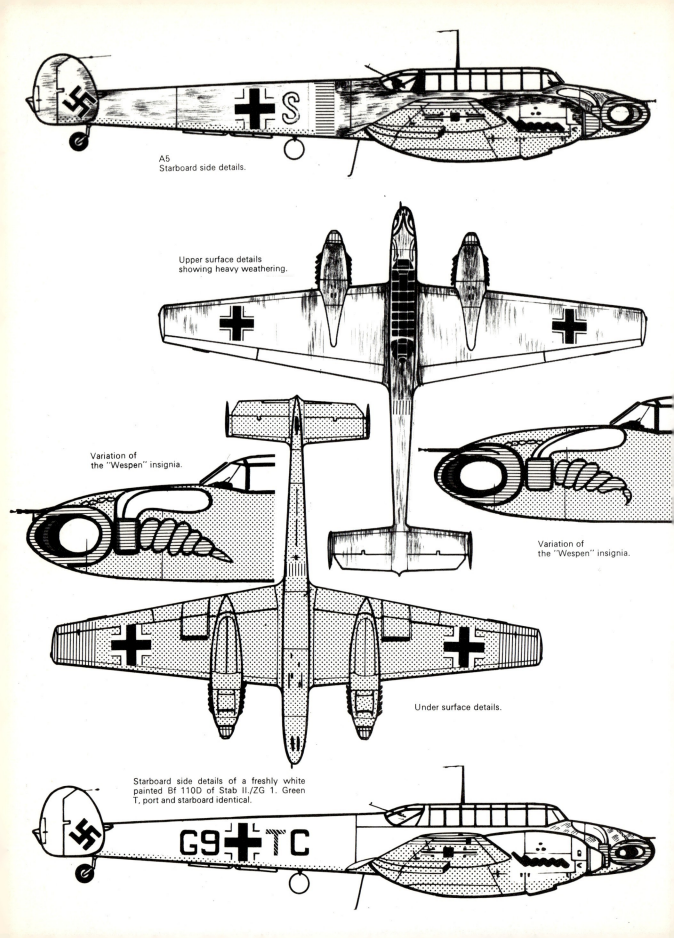

A Bf 110E of ZG 1 receiving the yellow, black, red and white "Wasp" insignia.

Above: A pair of Bf 110D-3's of 9./ZG 26 with 198 gallon drop-tanks, Mediterranean area, 1941. Note white tip to fuselage aft of tail-plane.

Above: Another Bf 110D-3 of 9./ZG 26 on a Sicilian airfield, 1941.
Below: Three-quarter rear view of the Bf 110D-3 illustrated in the heading photograph on the title page. Note white tip to end of fuselage.

Above & below: Bf 110C-2 of 3./ZG 26 showing off late 1940 markings, white nose, spinners and fuselage band; note the aircraft letter has been overpainted on the under surfaces.

Below: Heavily dappled Bf 110E-1 of II./ZG 26.

Above: A Bf 110C of I./ZG 52 showing off the white dragon on black shield insignia sometime during 1939–40.

Above: An over-all matt black Bf 110G of 6./NJG 4. Code is 3C+AR, 3CR in grey, A in red outlined white.

Below: Bf 110E-2 of 1./NJG 3 in over-all matt black night fighter scheme, Mediterranean, summer 1941. Note insignia below front cockpit.

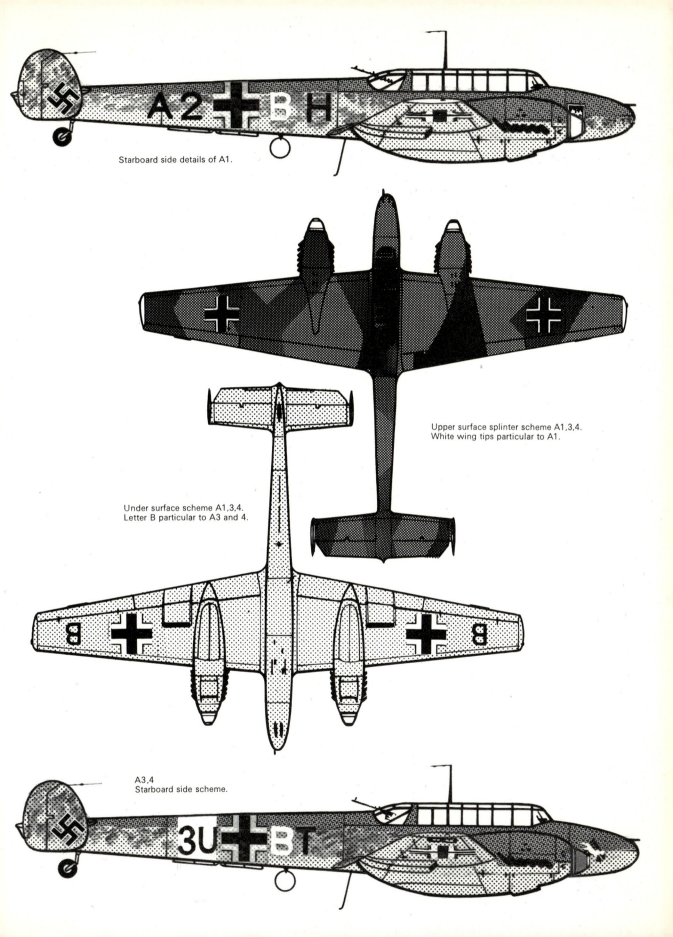

Starboard side details of A1.

Upper surface splinter scheme A1,3,4. White wing tips particular to A1.

Under surface scheme A1,3,4. Letter B particular to A3 and 4.

A3,4 Starboard side scheme.

Hs 123A-1's of 8./Sch.G.1 bombed up on a Russian airfield during the summer of 1942. All aircraft are in black green upper surface finish. Note the undercarriage fairings have all been removed.

Close-up of the "Infanterie-Sturmbzeichen" close support insignia on the fuselage of a Hs 123A-1 of 8./Sch.G.1 on the East Front, 1942.

Hs 123A-1 of an unidentified unit in Russia during the winter of 1942–43.

Formation of Hs 123A-1's of II./SG 2 taking off from a Russian airfield probably in 1944, the Adjutant's aircraft is nearest the camera.

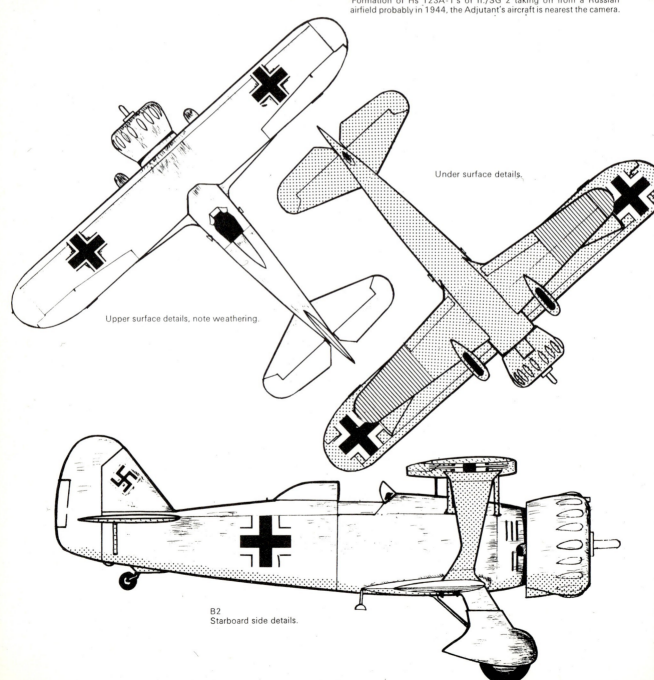

Upper surface details, note weathering.

Under surface details.

B2
Starboard side details.

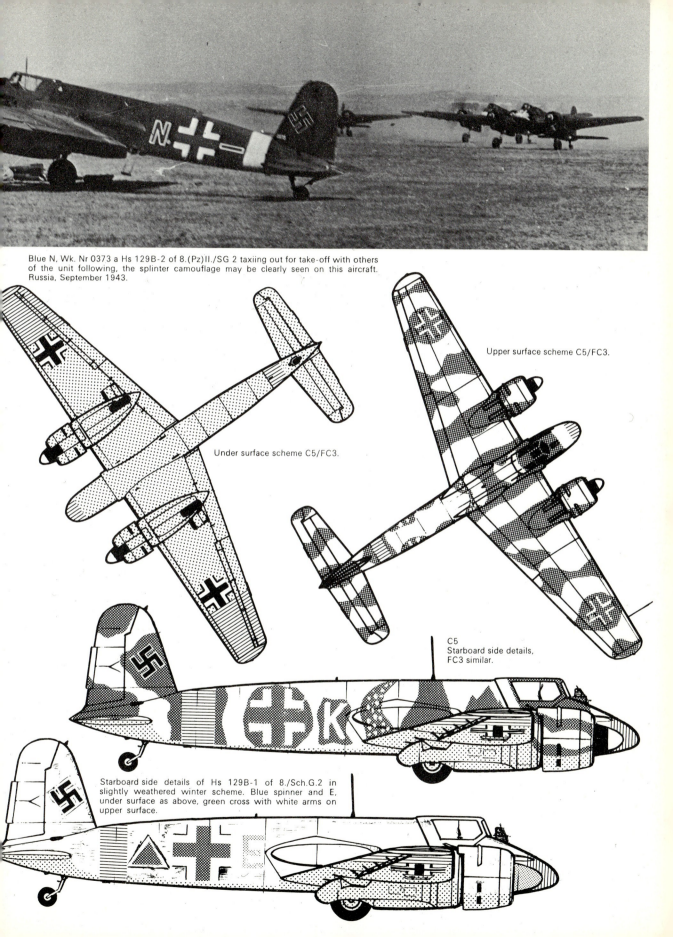

Blue N, Wk. Nr 0373 a Hs 129B-2 of 8.(Pz)II./SG 2 taxiing out for take-off with others of the unit following, the splinter camouflage may be clearly seen on this aircraft. Russia, September 1943.

Under surface scheme C5/FC3.

Upper surface scheme C5/FC3.

C5 Starboard side details, FC3 similar.

Starboard side details of Hs 129B-1 of 8./Sch.G.2 in slightly weathered winter scheme. Blue spinner and E, under surface as above, green cross with white arms on upper surface.

Above: Armourers working on a Hs 129B-2/R2 of IV(Pz)./SG 9. Russia, March 1944. Note the airscrews have also been daubed with white.

Above & below: Port and starboard shots of B and K of IV(Pz)./SG 9.

Fw 189A-2 of 1(H)./32 on a snow covered airfield in the White Sea area during 1942. The Staffel insignia may be discerned beneath the cockpit.

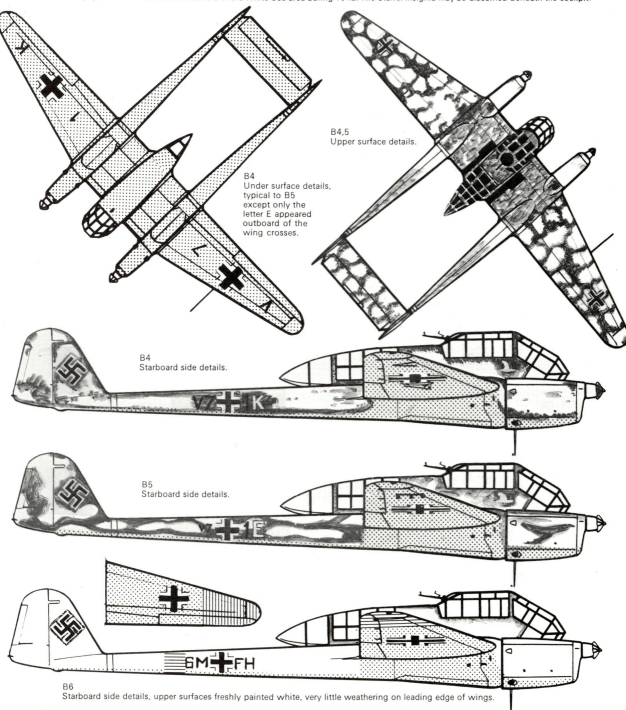

B4
Under surface details, typical to B5 except only the letter E appeared outboard of the wing crosses.

B4,5
Upper surface details.

B4
Starboard side details.

B5
Starboard side details.

B6
Starboard side details, upper surfaces freshly painted white, very little weathering on leading edge of wings.

Above: Fine flying shot of a Fw 189A-2 of 1(H)./31; a close inspection of the photograph reveals no splinter pattern on the upper surfaces. Code is 5D+MH.

Above & below: Port and starboard shots of 5D+EH with her port undercarriage through the ice crust. Note the heavily weathered appearance of this aircraft and that the port wing is devoid of snow camouflage. Note twin 7.9mm MG 81 machine guns in dorsal position. Fw 189A-2 of 1(H)./31.

Excellent detail shots of a Fw 189A-2 of 1(H)./32 being readied for an armed recce mission. Note the grey goose Staffel insignia beneath cockpit.

Above: Ju 87B's of I./St.G. 1 heading westwards along the Libyan coast. Note the white aircraft letter on the upper surfaces of the wing, repeated in black on the under surfaces. The nearest aircraft, A5+BH is in splinter scheme.

Below: A sand with green dapple camouflaged Ju 87B of St.G 3, Mediterranean area. Note the legend "Wasser" on the cowl in foreground.

Below: Formation of Ju 87B's of 4./St.G 2 "Immelmann" heading out on a ground attack mission. Note the Afrika Korps palm insignia on the cowl. Code of nearest aircraft is T6+BM.

Above: Ju 87D-3 of Stab II./St.G 2 "Immelmann", note Kommandeurs chevron. Middle and below Ju 87B-3's of the same unit.

Ju 87D-3's of I./St.G 2 showing a variety of camouflage schemes, Russian front.

Above: A pair of snow camouflaged Ju 87D-3's of St.G 5 during the winter of 1942–43 in Russia.

Above: A freshly painted Ju 87D-3 being bombed-up, and below, port side shots of the two aircraft illustrated at top of page.

Above: Formation of Ju 87D-3's of 4./St.G. 77, code of nearest aircraft is S2+NM.

Above: Yellow cowled Ju 87B-2's of 5./St.G. 77 taxiing in on a Balkan airfield during early spring 1941.
Below: Ju 87B-2's of 7./St.G. 77, note the extended fuses on the SC 250 bombs.

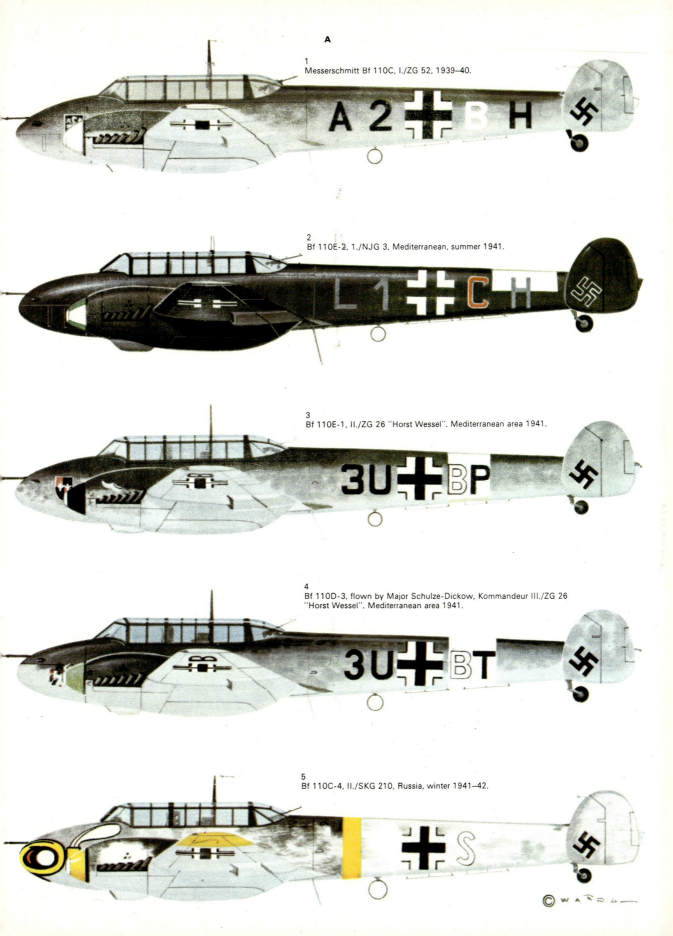

A

1
Messerschmitt Bf 110C, I./ZG 52, 1939–40.

2
Bf 110E-2, 1./NJG 3, Mediterranean, summer 1941.

3
Bf 110E-1, II./ZG 26 "Horst Wessel". Mediterranean area 1941.

4
Bf 110D-3, flown by Major Schulze-Dickow, Kommandeur III./ZG 26 "Horst Wessel". Mediterranean area 1941.

5
Bf 110C-4, II./SKG 210, Russia, winter 1941–42.

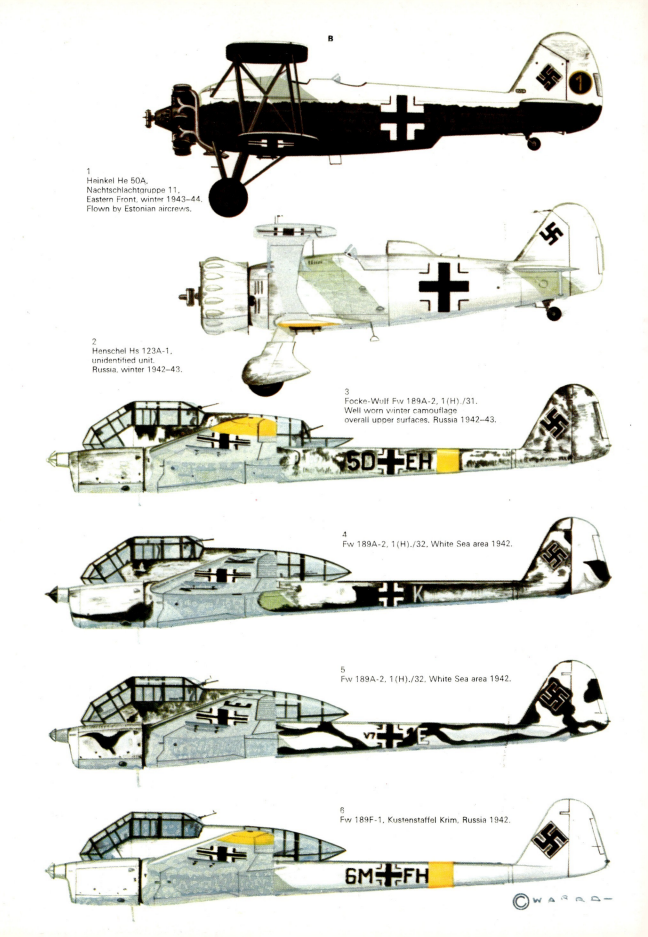

1
Heinkel He 50A,
Nachtschlachtgruppe 11,
Eastern Front, winter 1943–44.
Flown by Estonian aircrews.

2
Henschel Hs 123A-1,
unidentified unit,
Russia, winter 1942–43.

3
Focke-Wulf Fw 189A-2, 1(H)./31.
Well worn winter camouflage
overall upper surfaces. Russia 1942–43.

4
Fw 189A-2, 1(H)./32, White Sea area 1942.

5
Fw 189A-2, 1(H)./32, White Sea area 1942.

6
Fw 189F-1, Kustenstaffel Krim, Russia 1942.

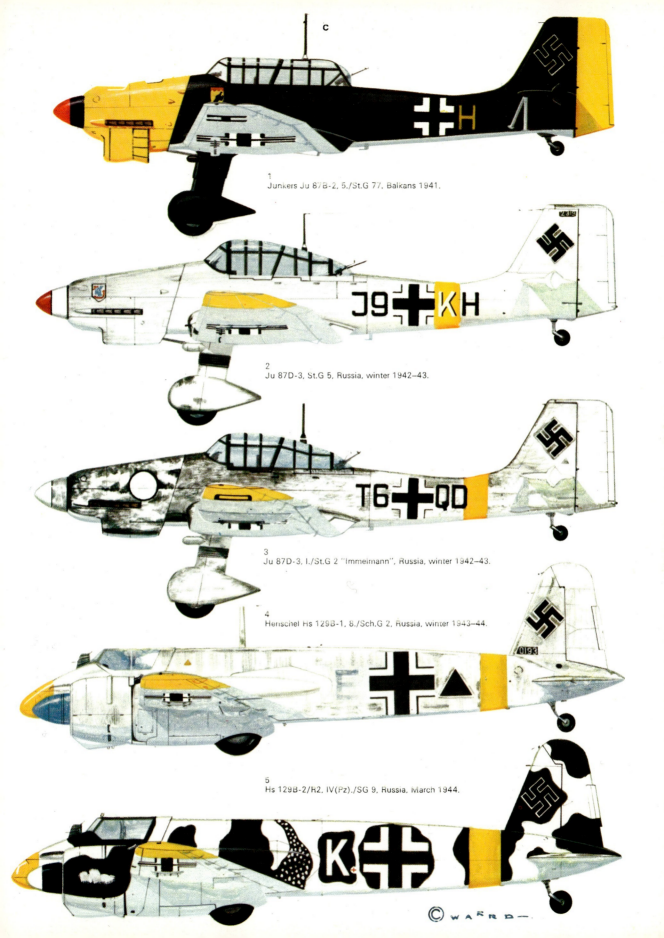

1 Junkers Ju 87B-2, 5./St.G 77, Balkans 1941.

2 Ju 87D-3, St.G 5, Russia, winter 1942–43.

3 Ju 87D-3, I./St.G 2 "Immelmann", Russia, winter 1942–43.

4 Henschel Hs 129B-1, 8./Sch.G 2, Russia, winter 1943–44.

5 Hs 129B-2/R2, IV(Pz)./SG 9, Russia, March 1944.

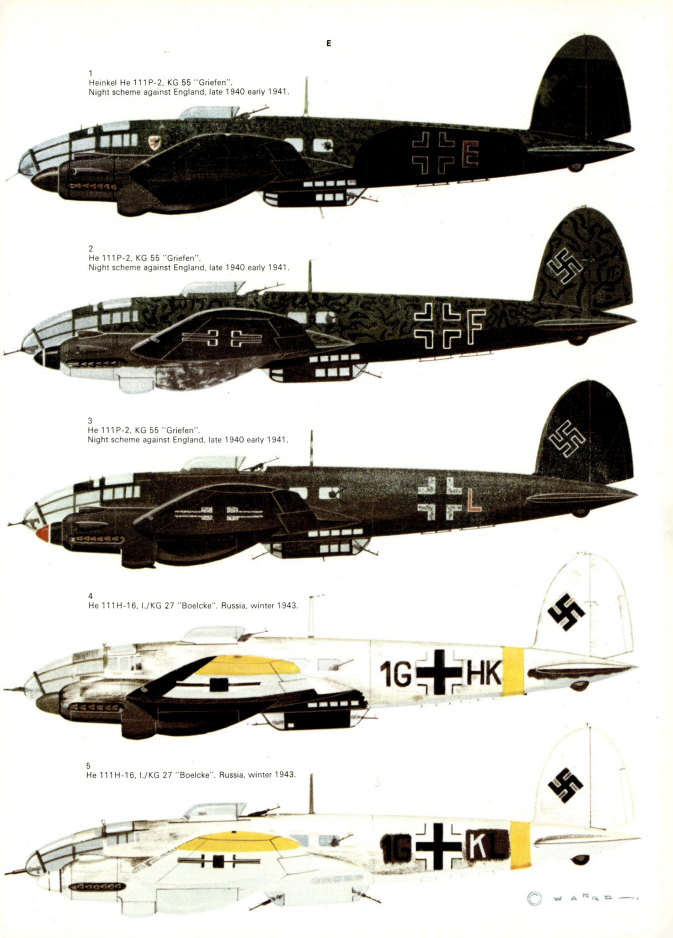

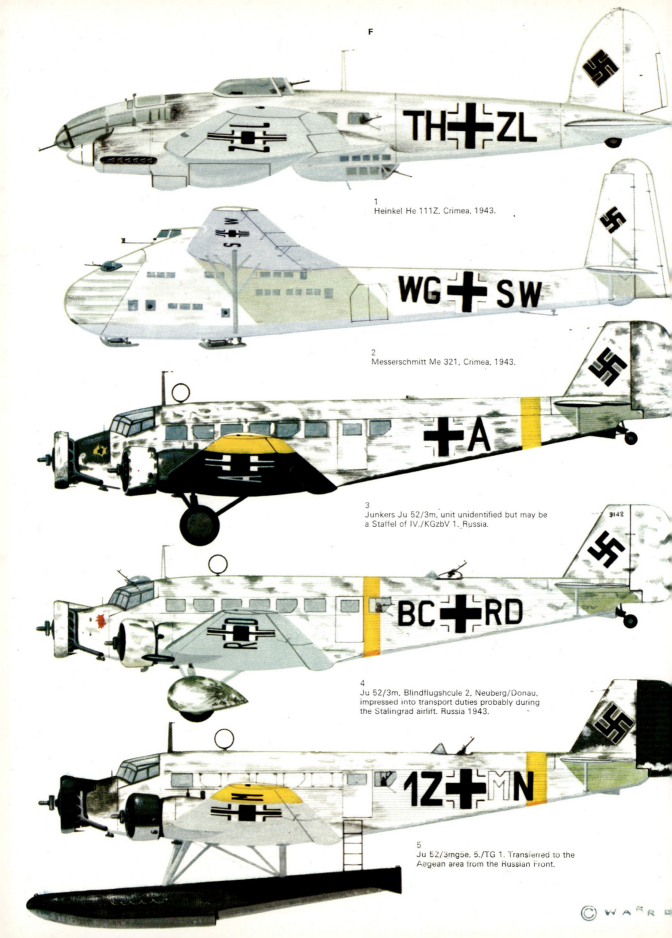

1
Heinkel He 111Z, Crimea, 1943.

2
Messerschmitt Me 321, Crimea, 1943.

3
Junkers Ju 52/3m, unit unidentified but may be a Staffel of IV./KGzbV 1. Russia.

4
Ju 52/3m, Blindflugshcule 2, Neuberg/Donau, impressed into transport duties probably during the Stalingrad airlift. Russia 1943.

5
Ju 52/3mg5e. 5./TG 1. Transferred to the Aegean area from the Russian Front.

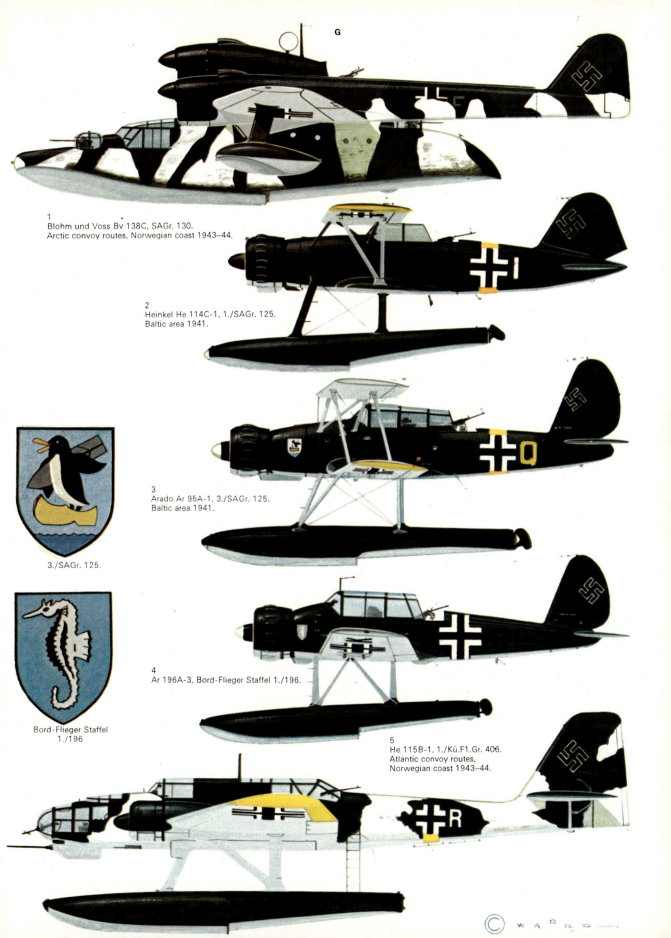

1
Blohm und Voss Bv 138C, SAGr. 130.
Arctic convoy routes, Norwegian coast 1943–44.

2
Heinkel He 114C-1, 1./SAGr. 125.
Baltic area 1941.

3
Arado Ar 95A-1, 3./SAGr. 125.
Baltic area 1941.

3./SAGr. 125.

Bord-Flieger Staffel
1./196

4
Ar 196A-3, Bord-Flieger Staffel 1./196.

5
He 115B-1, 1./Kü.Fl.Gr. 406.
Atlantic convoy routes,
Norwegian coast 1943–44.

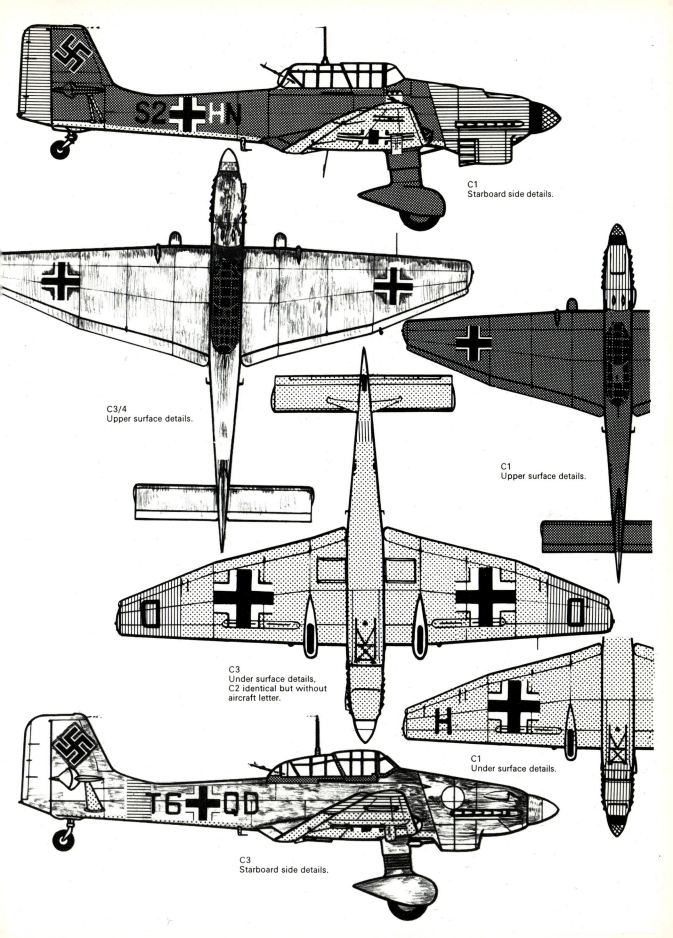

Above: A peculiarly dappled Ju 88A-14 of 1./KG 77 operating from Sicilian airfields on anti-shipping strikes, note the 20mm cannon in the nose gondola.

Above: Ju 88A-4 of III./KG 3 "Blitz".
Below: Snow camouflaged Ju 88A-4 of KG 3, Wk. Nr 9568 on fin and nose.

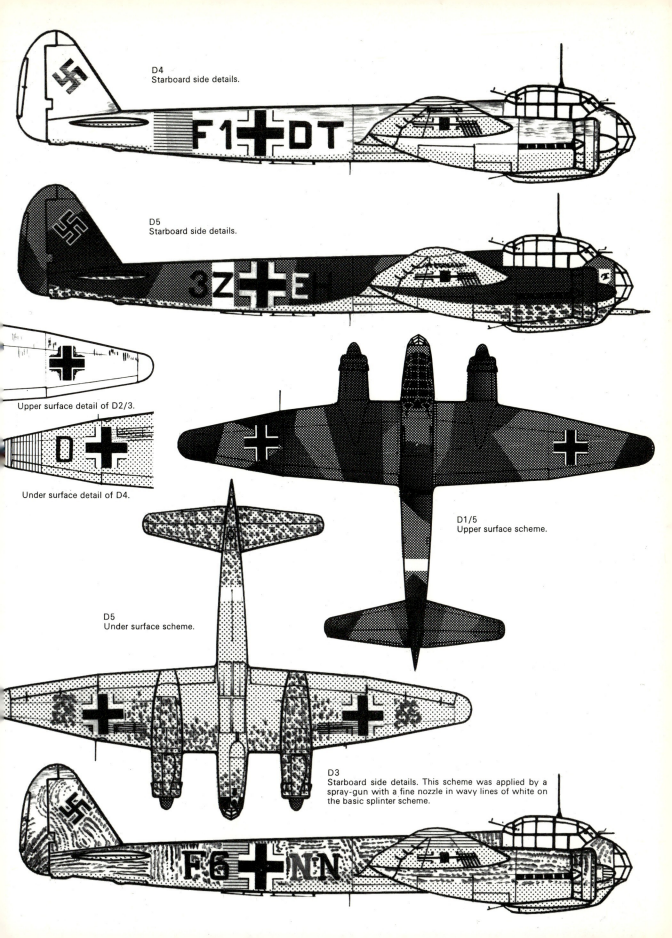

Above: He 111P-6 of KG 55 "Griefen" in black green upper surfaces with all under surfaces roughly blacked in, late 1940 early 1941.

Below: He 111P-2's of KG 55 in the hastily adopted night camouflage of late 1940, each of the four aircraft illustrated show variations in the extent of the matt black.

Below: He 111H-16 of I./KG 27 in winter scheme on a bombing mission over the Eastern Front during 1943.

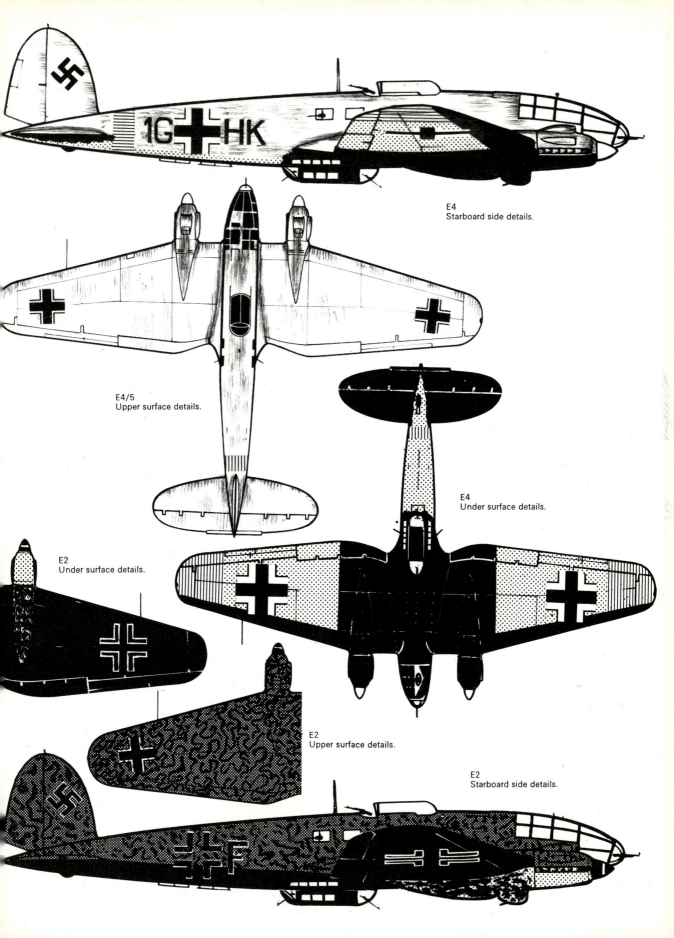

E4 Starboard side details.

E4/5 Upper surface details.

E4 Under surface details.

E2 Under surface details.

E2 Upper surface details.

E2 Starboard side details.

Above: With the "devils head" insignia on the nose this Ju 52 in winter camouflage with night under surfaces on the Eastern Front may belong to a Staffel of IV./KGzbV 1.

Below: A Ju 52/3m of III./KGzbV 1 on the Palermo–Tunis run, black under surfaces, splinter upper surfaces.

Below: With black and white striped cowls Ju 52/3m's of KGrzb V head out over the Mediterranean. Nearest aircraft is coded 7V (black outlined white)+C (yellow)J(white). Splinter upper surfaces, standard under surfaces, white J outboard of cross.

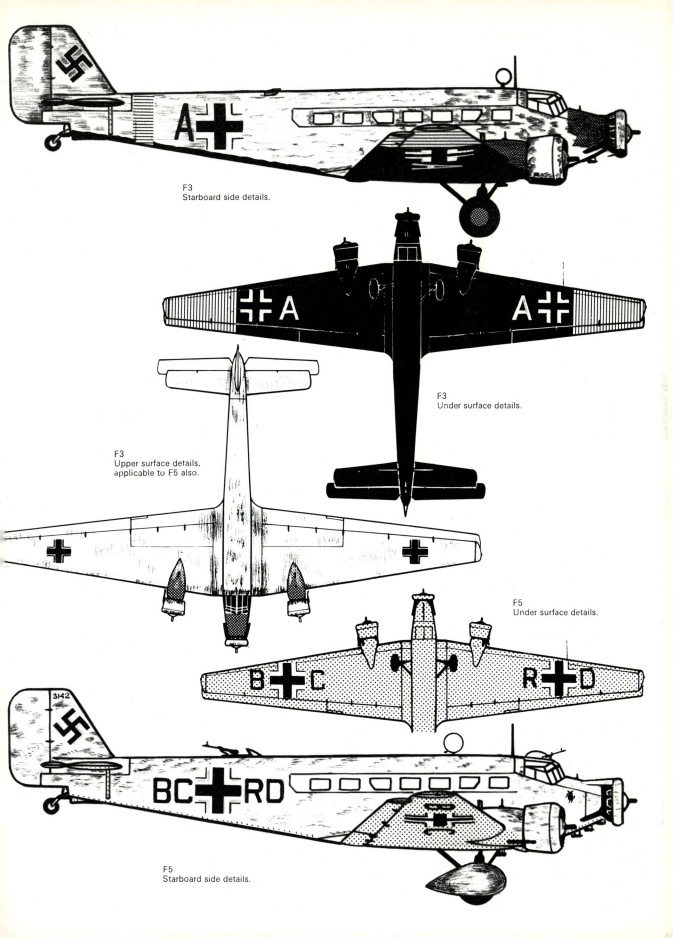

F3 Starboard side details.

F3 Under surface details.

F3 Upper surface details, applicable to F5 also.

F5 Under surface details.

F5 Starboard side details.

Above: Excellent detail shot of the upper surfaces of a Do 24 being winched ashore, upper surfaces are in splinter scheme, probably photographed in early 1940.

Below: A pair of Do 24T-1's of an unidentified unit, the reindeer head indicates operations in northern latitudes. Upper surfaces in black green.

A Mediterranean based Do 24T-1, code is KK+UP.

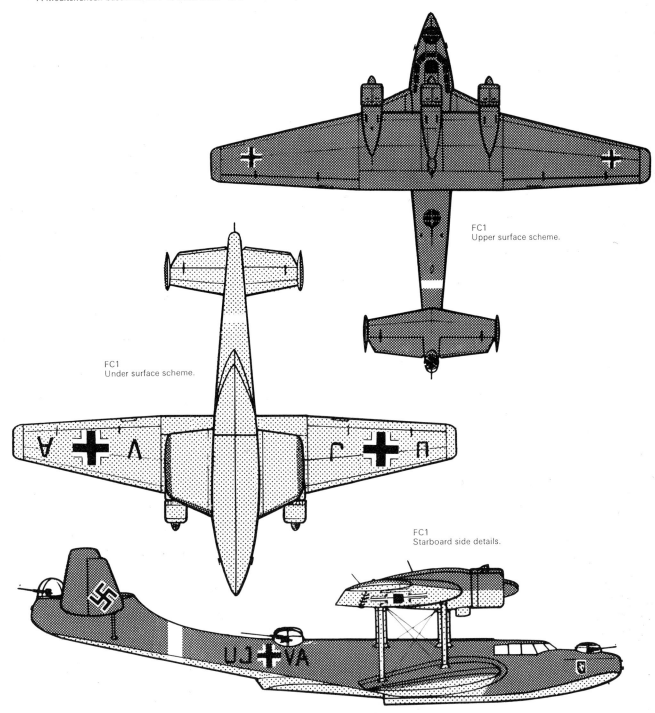

FC1 Upper surface scheme.

FC1 Under surface scheme.

FC1 Starboard side details.

Above: Bv 138C, taxiing in to rendezvous with a U-boat after a patrol over the Arctic convoy routes.

Above & below: The same aircraft rendezvousing at different times with U-boats, Norwegian coast 1943–44 winter. Note radar array on leading edge of wings.

Another Bv 138C tied up to a U-boat at sun-down.

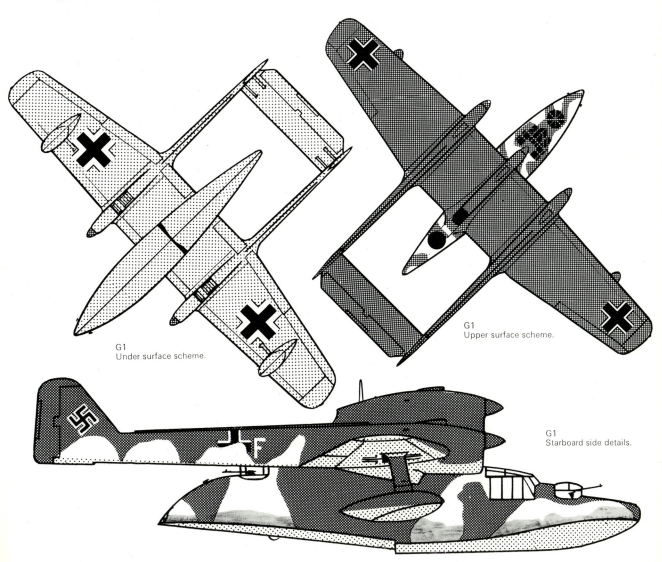

G1
Under surface scheme.

G1
Upper surface scheme.

G1
Starboard side details.

Above: He 115B-1 of 1./Kü.Fl.Gr 406 ashore for overhaul in a Norwegian fjord during 1943, code is K6+RH.

Below: K6+TH, another He 115B-1 of the same unit, after having both floats replaced. These aircraft operated over the Arctic convoy routes during the winter of 1943–44.

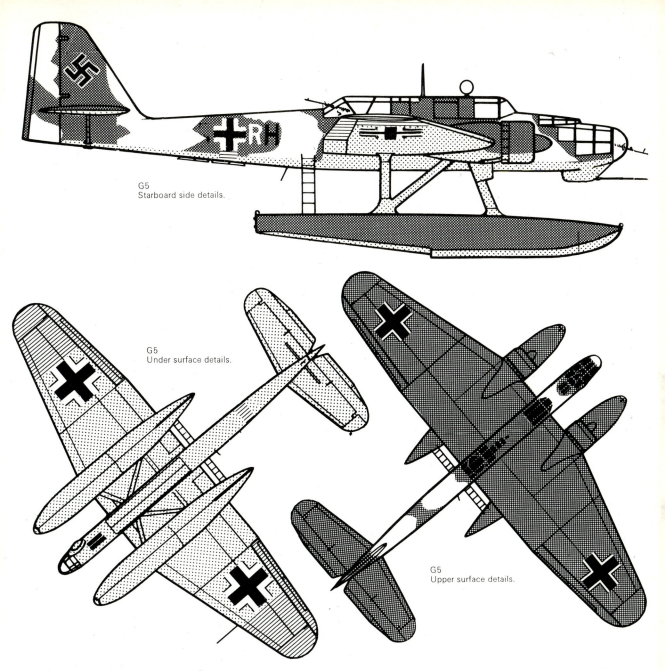

G5 Starboard side details.

G5 Under surface details.

G5 Upper surface details.

Port side view of K6+RH, clearly shown is the yellow wing tip and fuselage band below the cross. Note 20mm MG 151..

Ju 53/3mg5e of 5./TG 1 taking off from an Aegean base on a supply mission, camouflage is of course Russian winter scheme. Code 1Z+MN.

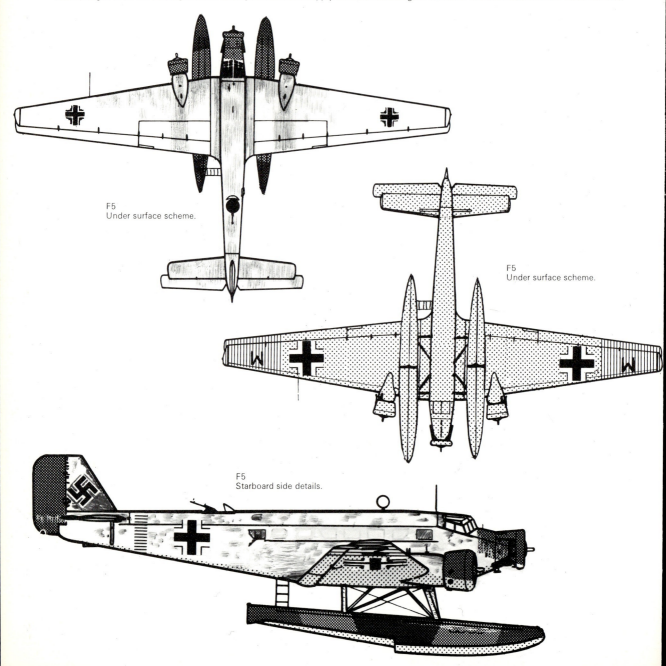

F5
Under surface scheme.

F5
Under surface scheme.

F5
Starboard side details.

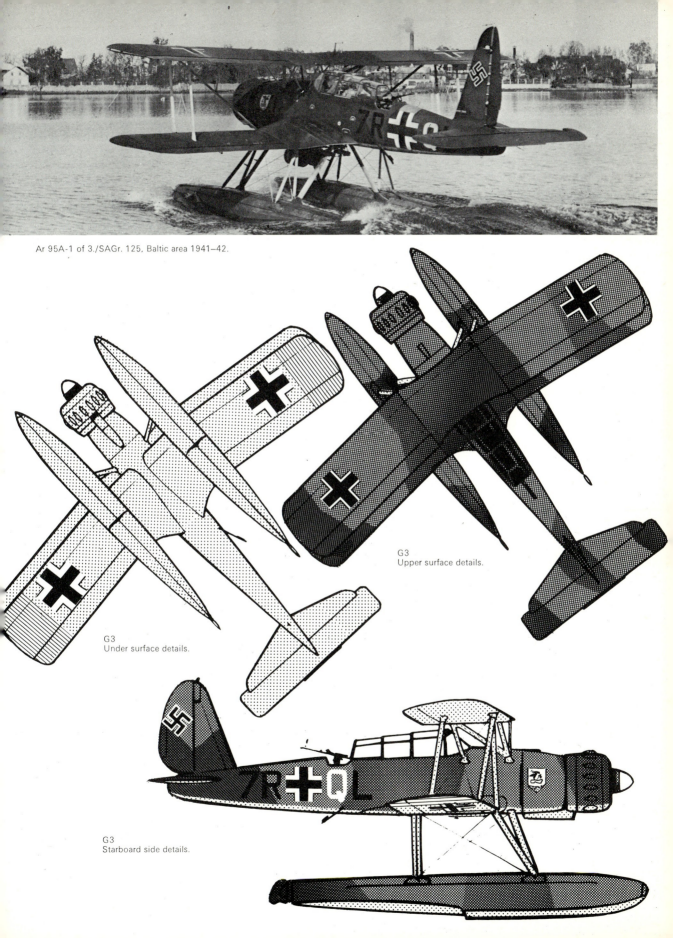

Ar 95A-1 of 3./SAGr. 125, Baltic area 1941–42.

G3
Under surface details.

G3
Upper surface details.

G3
Starboard side details.

He 114C-1 of 1./SAGr. 125, Baltic area 1941. Note white tips to floats.

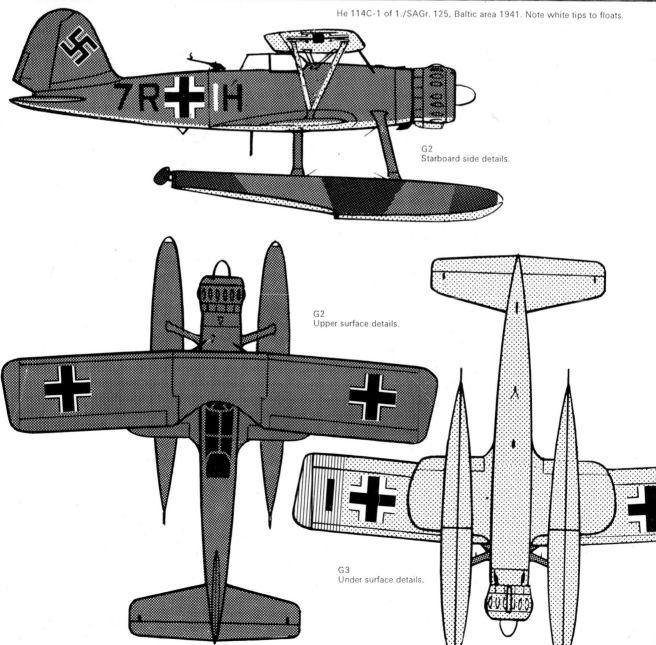

G2 Starboard side details.

G2 Upper surface details.

G3 Under surface details.